W9-CSJ-517

Mel Bay's Modern
GUITAR METHOD
GRADE 1
Expanded Edition

The **Modern Guitar Method Grade 1** is the world's premier course of instruction. This expanded version presents extra playing material which will help the student master various technical concepts.

For additional study, I highly recommend **First Lessons Beginning Guitar: Learning Chords Playing Songs** Book/CD set (20000BCD). Also, for additional playing material in all styles, I would highly recommend, **Mastering the Guitar Volume 1A** Book/CD set (96620BCD)

CD Contents

Tk	Pg	Title		Tk	Pg	Title		Tk	Pg	Title	
1		Tuning	[1:38]	28	52	Chord Studies in C	[1:25]	50	74	In the Evening by the	
2	17	Sunset	[0:49]	29	53	A Daily Scale Study;				Moonlight	[0:51]
3	17	Aura Lee	[0:50]			Running Around	[1:21]	51	74	Etude	[0:56]
4	22	Cockles and Mussels	[0:36]	30	54	Home, Home, Can I		52	75	The Old Mill	[0:38]
5	22	Hymn	[0:33]			Forget Thee	[0:54]	53	75	Two-Four Picking	[0:25]
6	22	German Waltz	[0:20]	31	54	Long, Long Ago	[1:09]	54	76	A Scale Study	[1:18]
7	25	Amazing Grace	[0:39]	32	59	Playtime	[0:57]	55	76	Opening Day	[1:14]
8	25	Tenting Tonight	[0:59]	33	61	Accompaniment Styles		56	76	A Serenade	[1:08]
9	25	Melancholy	[0:41]			in A Minor;		57	77	Austrian Hymn	[1:11]
10	28	Elsie's Waltz	[0:18]			Orchestration Style;		58	77	Home on the Range	[1:06]
11	28	Buffalo Gals	[0:39]			Chord Studies in the		59	78	The Little Prince	[0:48]
12	28	Chester	[0:36]			Key of A Minor	[2:16]	60	78	Carry Me Back to	
13	30	Mountain Flower	[0:30]	34	63	Picking Study in Am	[1:31]			Old Virginny	[1:36]
14	30	Quest	[0:27]	35	64	Sailing	[0:32]	61	79	Picking Studies	[1:11]
15	30	Homeward Bound	[0:22]	36	64	Minor Song	[0:25]	62	80	Picking Studies	[2:06]
16	31	Daydreams; Ozark		37	64	Journey	[0:28]	63	81	Chord Studies	[2:18]
		Stream; Waterfall;		38	65	Wayfaring Stranger	[0:38]	64	82	Cindy	[0:33]
		Mountain Trail	[1:41]	39	66	Careless Love	[1:18]	65	82	Night Song	[1:13]
17	35	Smoky Ridge	[0:31]	40	67	Foggy Mountain Run	[0:50]	66	83	East River	[1:07]
18	35	Voyage	[0:42]	41	67	The Shire	[0:25]	67	83	Goblins	[0:53]
19	36	Our First Duet	[0:39]	42	67	Bluegrass Sunrise	[0:20]	68	84	Lament	[2:00]
20	36	The Repeater	[0:31]	43	68	Cradle Song	[1:04]	69	85	Maytime	[1:00]
21	37	Two Guitars	[0:37]	44	69	Billy's Duet	[1:24]	70	86	Rondo	[1:14]
22	37	Sunset	[0:39]	45	69	Lafayette Square	[1:03]	71	87	Sor's Waltz	[1:22]
23	43	Follow the Leader	[0:48]	46	70	Song Without Words	[0:56]	72	87	Bluegrass Waltz	[0:30]
24	43	Tallis Canon	[0:23]	47	70	Terry's Tune	[1:34]	73	88	Running the Thirds in G	[0:22]
25	48	Scale/Picking Studies	[1:48]	48	71	A Daily Drill; Picking		74	88	A Little Bit of Hanon	[0:45]
26	49	Shenandoah Valley				Studies in G	[2:44]	75	88	Southern Fried	[0:27]
		(easy and advanced)	[2:28]	49	73	Accompaniment Styles					
27	50	Blue Bells of Scotland				in the Key of G	[1:59]				
		(easy and advanced)	[2:10]								

5 6 7 8 9 0

© 1948 (Renewed) 1972, 1975, 1980, 1990, 2005 BY MEL BAY PUBLICATIONS, INC., PACIFIC, MO 63069.

Visit us on the Web at www.melbay.com — E-mail us at email@melbay.com

The correct way to hold the guitar.

 Tr. 2 #1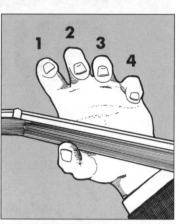

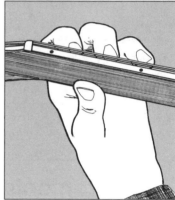

#2

Place your fingers
FIRMLY on the strings
DIRECTLY BEHIND
THE FRETS.

#1

This is the pick.

#2

Hold it in this
manner firmly
between the thumb
and first finger.

#3

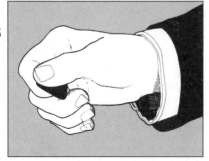

$\sqcap$ = **DOWN STROKE OF THE PICK.**

#4

2

The six open strings of the guitar will be of the same pitch as the six notes shown in the illustration of the piano keyboard. Note that five of the strings are below the middle C of the piano keyboard.

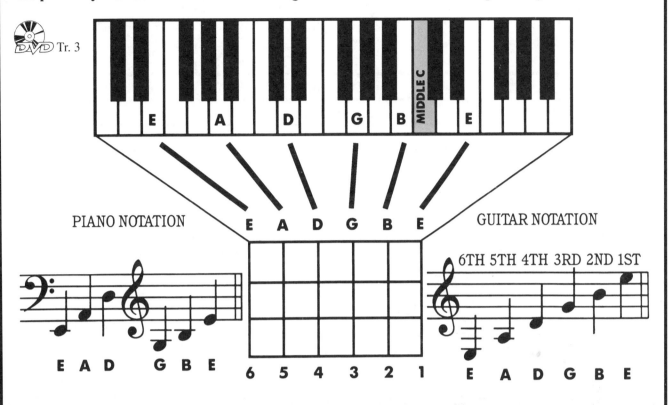

Tr. 3

PIANO NOTATION

GUITAR NOTATION

E A D G B E

6TH 5TH 4TH 3RD 2ND 1ST

6 5 4 3 2 1

E A D G B E

E A D G B E

ANOTHER METHOD OF TUNING

1. Tune the 6th string in unison with the **E** or 12th white key to the LEFT of MIDDLE C on the piano.

2. Place the finger behind the fifth fret of the 6th string. This will give you the tone or pitch of the 5th string **(A)**.

3. Place finger behind the fifth fret of the 5th string to get the pitch of the 4th string **(D)**.

4. Repeat same procedure to obtain the pitch of the 3rd string **(G)**.

5. Place finger behind the fourth fret of the 3rd string to get the pitch of the 2nd string **(B)**.

6. Place finger behind the fifth fret of the 2nd string to get the pitch of the 1st string **(E)**.

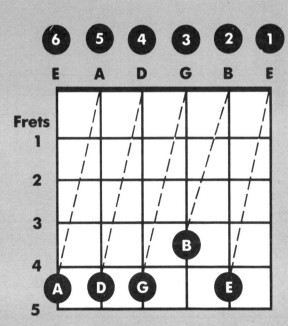

ELECTRONIC GUITAR TUNER

 Tr. 4 - Tune up

Electronic Guitar Tuners are available at your music store. They are a handy device and highly recommended.

THE RUDIMENTS OF MUSIC

THE STAFF:

Music is written on a STAFF consisting of FIVE LINES and FOUR SPACES. The lines and spaces are numbered upward as shown:

```
5TH LINE ─────────────────────────────────────────
                           4TH SPACE
4TH LINE ─────────────────────────────────────────
                           3RD SPACE
3RD LINE ─────────────────────────────────────────
                           2ND SPACE
2ND LINE ─────────────────────────────────────────
                           1ST SPACE
1ST LINE ─────────────────────────────────────────
```

The lines and spaces are named after letters of the alphabet.

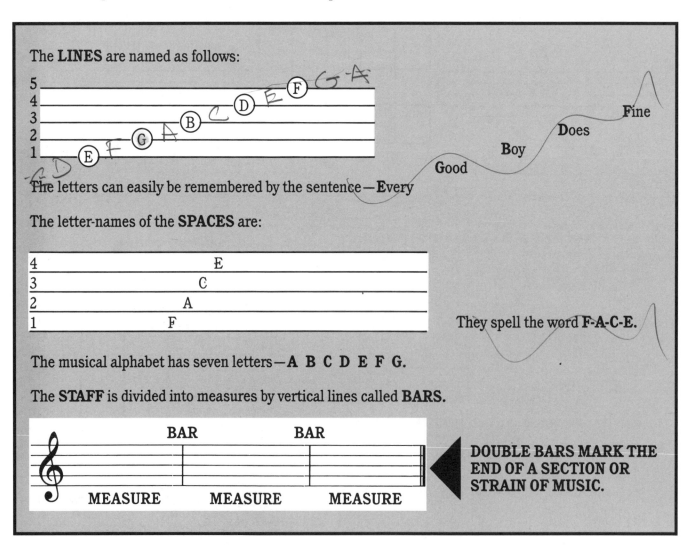

The **LINES** are named as follows:

The letters can easily be remembered by the sentence—**E**very **G**ood **B**oy **D**oes **F**ine

The letter-names of the **SPACES** are:

4	E
3	C
2	A
1	F

They spell the word **F-A-C-E**.

The musical alphabet has seven letters—**A B C D E F G**.

The **STAFF** is divided into measures by vertical lines called **BARS**.

BAR   BAR

MEASURE   MEASURE   MEASURE

◄ **DOUBLE BARS MARK THE END OF A SECTION OR STRAIN OF MUSIC.**

THE CLEF:

This sign is the treble or G clef.

All guitar music will be written in this clef.

The second line of the treble clef is known as the G line. Many people call the treble clef the G clef because it circles around the G line.

NOTES

THIS IS A NOTE: Tr. 5

A NOTE HAS THREE PARTS. THEY ARE

The HEAD
The STEM
The FLAG

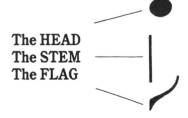

NOTES MAY BE PLACED IN THE STAFF,   ABOVE THE STAFF,

AND BELOW THE STAFF.

A note will bear the name of the line or space it occupies on the staff.
The location of a note in, above, or below the staff will indicate the pitch.

PITCH: the height or depth of a tone.
TONE: a musical sound.

TYPES OF NOTES

THE TYPE OF NOTE WILL
INDICATE THE LENGTH OF
ITS SOUND.

This is a whole note.
The head is hollow.
It does not have a stem.

$\mathbf{o}$ = 4 Beats
A whole note will receive
four beats or counts.

This is a half note.
The head is hollow.
It has a stem.

= 2 Beats
A half note will receive
two beats or counts.

This is a quarter note.
The head is solid.
It has a stem.

= 1 Beat
A quarter note will receive
one beat or count.

This is an eighth note.
The head is solid.
It has a stem and a flag.

= ½ Beat
An eighth note will receive
one-half beat or count.
(2 for 1 beat)

A REST is a sign used to designate a period of silence. This period of silence will be of the same duration of time as the note to which it corresponds.

 This is an eighth rest.

This is a quarter rest.

Half rest
Half rests lie on the line.

Whole rest
Whole rests hang down from the line.

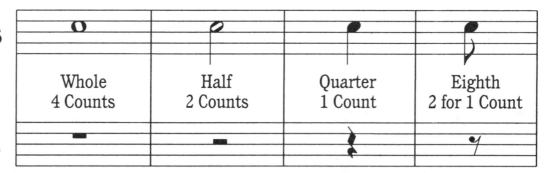

Notes	o	♩	●	♪
	Whole 4 Counts	Half 2 Counts	Quarter 1 Count	Eighth 2 for 1 Count
Rests	▬	▬	♩	7

THE TIME SIGNATURE

The above examples are the common types of time signatures to be used in this book.

The number of beats per measure. ▷ **4** ◁ Beats per measure

The type of note receiving one beat. ▷ **4** ◁ A quarter note receives one beat.

 Signifies so-called "common time" and is simply another way of designating 4/4 time.

Notes on the E String

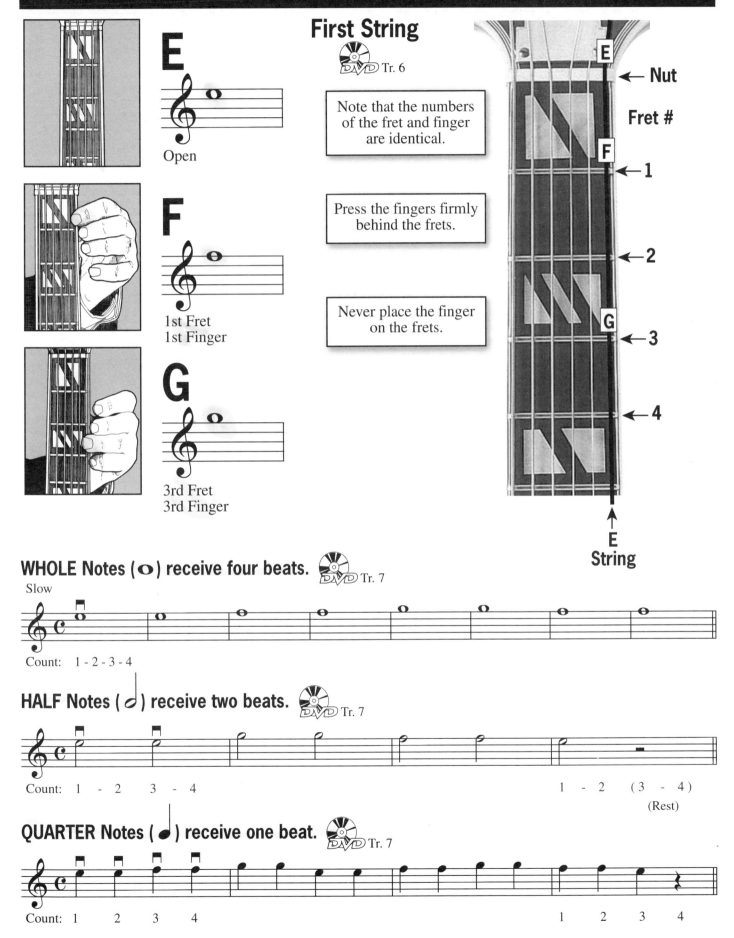

E — Open

F — 1st Fret, 1st Finger

G — 3rd Fret, 3rd Finger

First String
DVD Tr. 6

Note that the numbers of the fret and finger are identical.

Press the fingers firmly behind the frets.

Never place the finger on the frets.

E — Nut — Fret # — F — 1 — 2 — G — 3 — 4 — E String

WHOLE Notes (O) receive four beats. DVD Tr. 7

Slow

Count: 1 - 2 - 3 - 4

HALF Notes (d) receive two beats. DVD Tr. 7

Count: 1 - 2   3 - 4   1 - 2   (3 - 4)
                                                (Rest)

QUARTER Notes (♩) receive one beat. DVD Tr. 7

Count: 1   2   3   4   1   2   3   4

7

Playing the Notes  Tr. 8

Working the Fingers  Tr. 8

1st-String Etude  Tr. 9

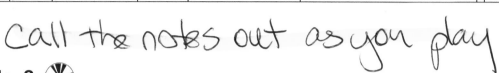

Call the notes out as you play

Etude No. 2 Tr. 9

The Mixmaster Tr. 9

Notes on the First String
(Fill in the blocks)

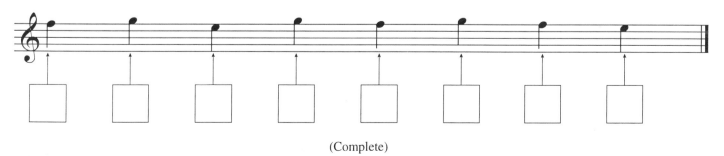

(Complete)

Notes on the B String

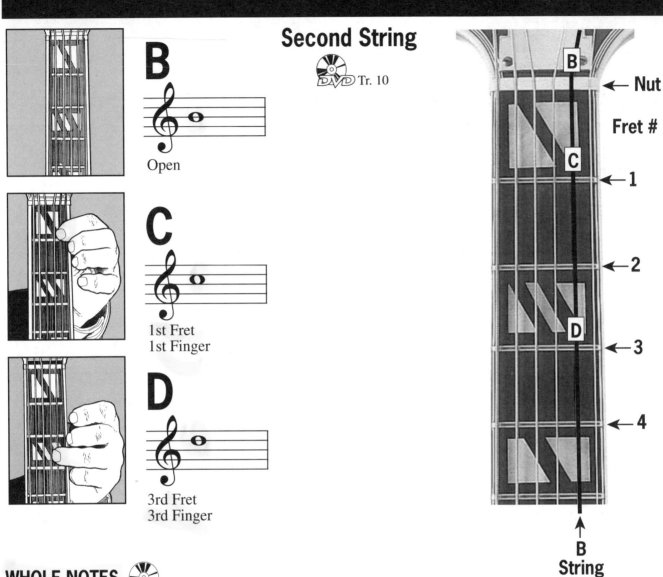

B
Open

C
1st Fret
1st Finger

D
3rd Fret
3rd Finger

Second String
Tr. 10

← Nut

Fret #

← 1

← 2

← 3

← 4

B String

WHOLE NOTES Tr. 10

Count: 1 - 2 - 3 - 4

HALF NOTES Tr. 10

Count: 1 - 2   3 - 4

QUARTER NOTES Tr. 10

Count: 1   2   3   4

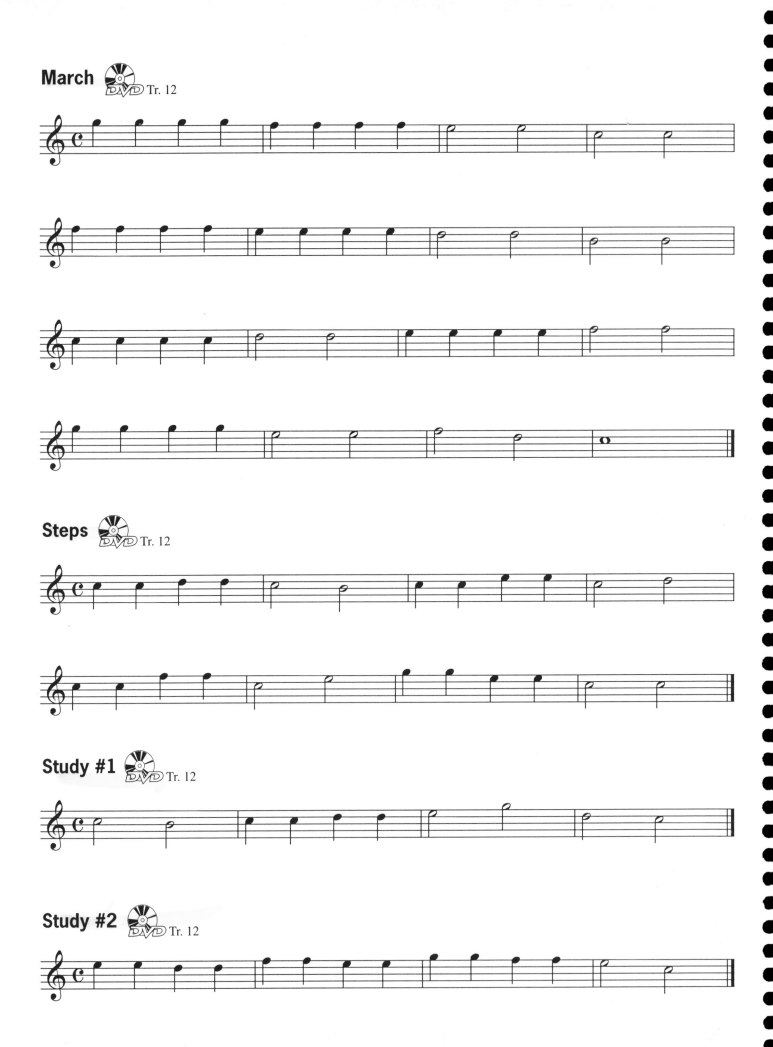

March Tr. 12

Steps Tr. 12

Study #1 Tr. 12

Study #2 Tr. 12

Inch Worm Tr. 13

Frolic Tr. 13

call the notes out as you play

E - B Tr. 13

Indian Drum Tr. 13

13

Three-Four Time

This sign 𝄞 3/4 indicates **three-four** time.

3 – beats per measure.
4 – type of note receiving one beat (quarter note).

In three-four time, we will have three beats per measure.

Dotted Half Notes

A dot (•) placed behind a note increases its value by one-half.

A dotted half note (𝅗𝅥•) will receive three beats.

Examples: 𝅗𝅥 = 2 counts   𝅗𝅥• = 3 counts

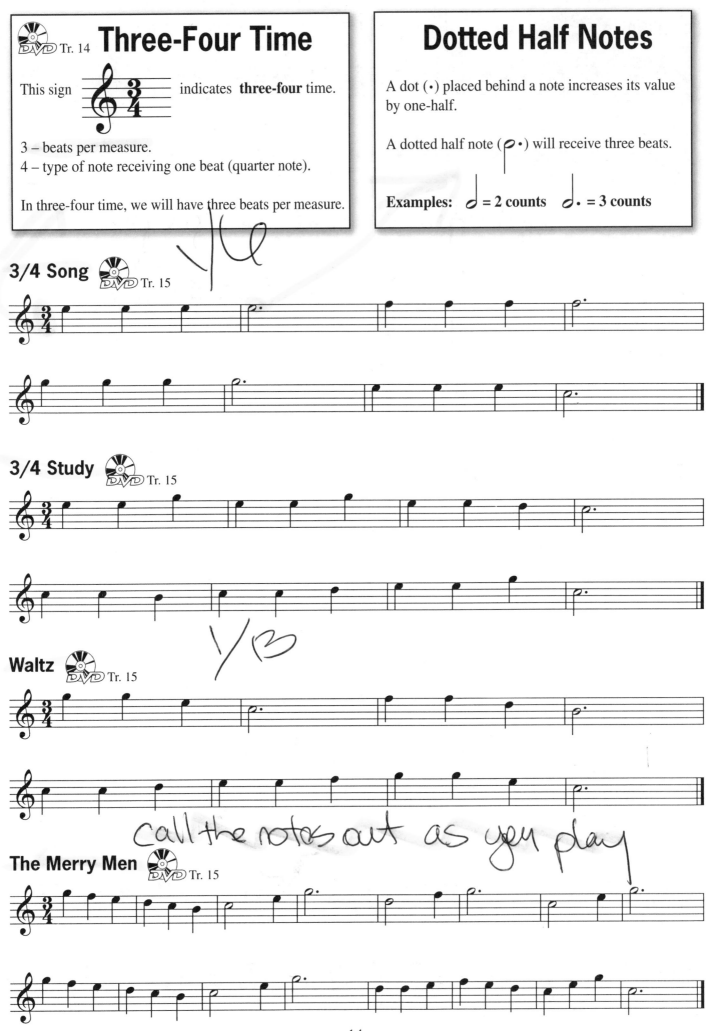

3/4 Song Tr. 15

3/4 Study Tr. 15

Waltz Tr. 15

The Merry Men Tr. 15

Notes on the G String

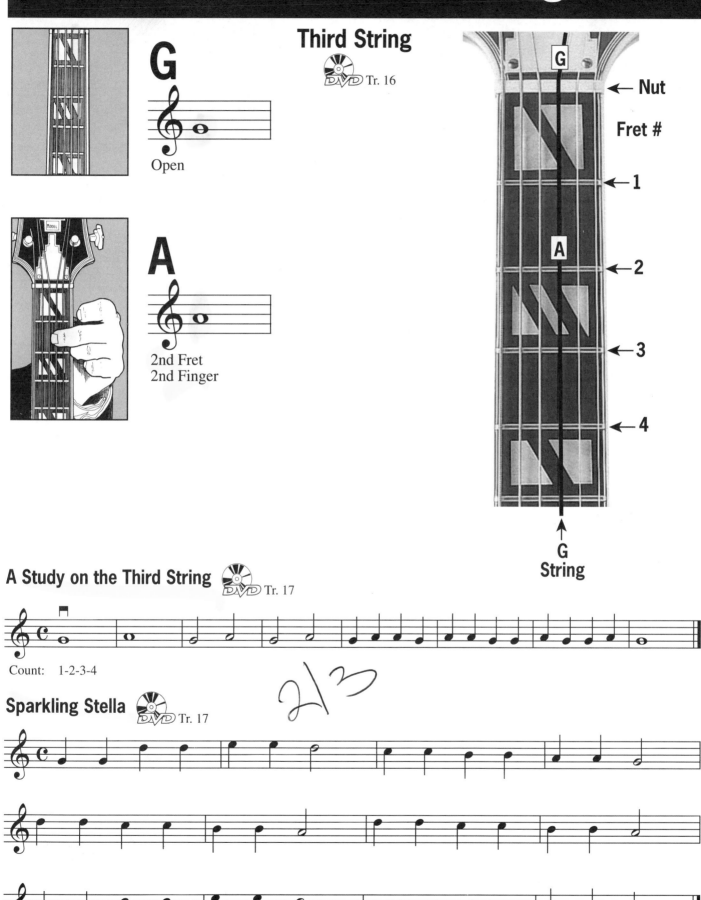

Third String DVD Tr. 16

G
Open

A
2nd Fret
2nd Finger

Nut

Fret #

← 1

← 2

← 3

← 4

G
String

A Study on the Third String DVD Tr. 17

Count: 1-2-3-4

2/3

Sparkling Stella DVD Tr. 17

15

Prelude  Tr. 18

Descending Tr. 18

Ascending Tr. 18

Sunset
Teacher Acc.  Tr. 2

Aura Lee
Teacher Acc. Tr. 3

Folk Song

17

Pick-Up Notes

One or more notes at the beginning of a strain before the first measure are referred to as **pick-up notes**.

The rhythm for pick-up notes is taken from the last measure of the selection and the beats are counted as such.

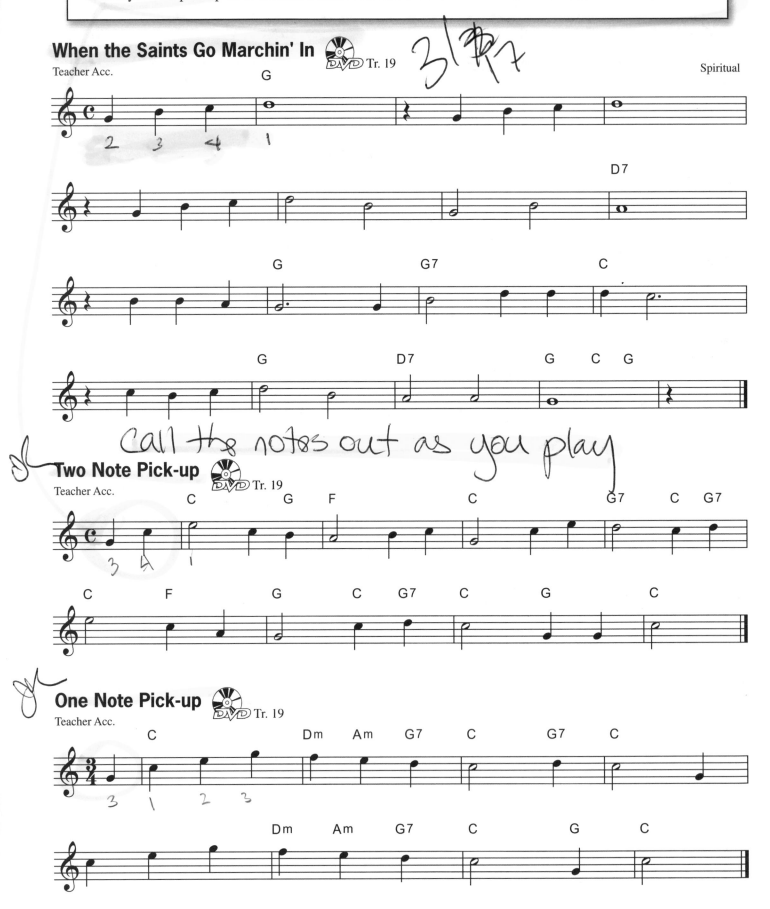

When the Saints Go Marchin' In   DVD Tr. 19

Teacher Acc.   Spiritual

Two Note Pick-up   DVD Tr. 19

Teacher Acc.

One Note Pick-up   DVD Tr. 19

Teacher Acc.

18

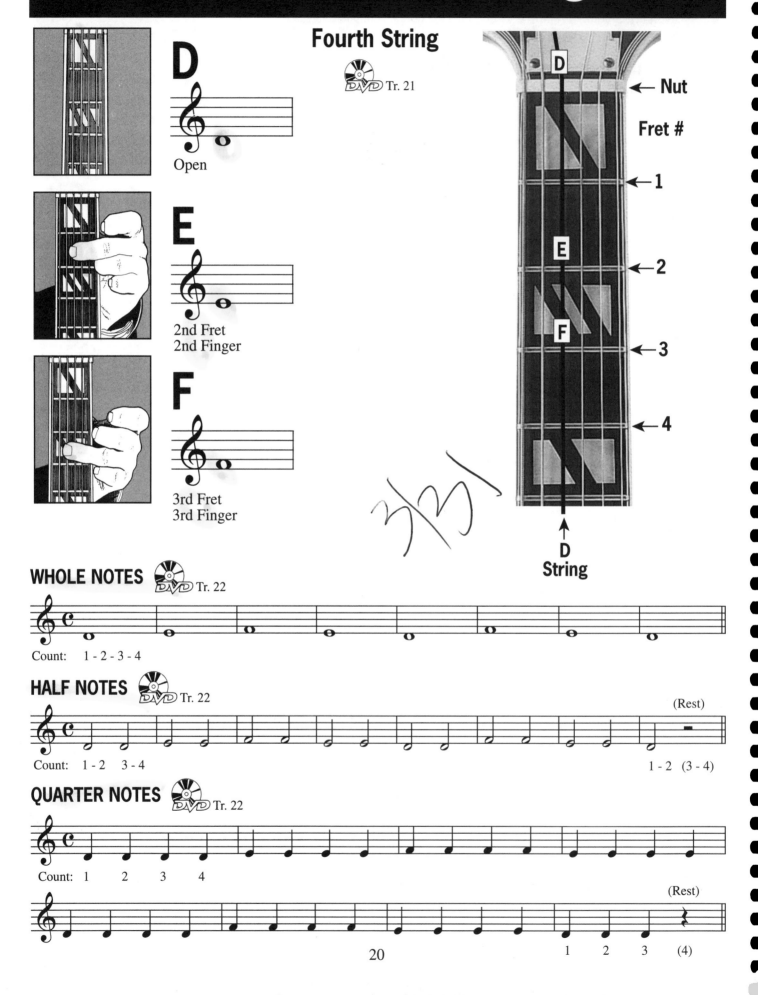

Notes on the D String

Fourth String

DVD Tr. 21

D Open

E 2nd Fret 2nd Finger

F 3rd Fret 3rd Finger

Nut

Fret #

1

2

3

4

D String

WHOLE NOTES DVD Tr. 22

Count: 1 - 2 - 3 - 4

HALF NOTES DVD Tr. 22

(Rest)

Count: 1 - 2   3 - 4

1 - 2   (3 - 4)

QUARTER NOTES DVD Tr. 22

Count: 1   2   3   4

(Rest)

1   2   3   (4)

4 String Note Review

21

Cockles and Mussels  Tr. 4

Teacher Acc.

Ballad

Hymn Tr. 5

Teacher Acc.

German Waltz Tr. 6

Teacher Acc.

The Eighth Note

 Tr. 24

An **eighth note** receives one-half beat. (One quarter note equals two eighth notes.)

An eighth note will have a head, stem, and flag. If two or more are in successive order, they may be connected by a beam. (See example.)

Eighth-Note Studies Tr. 25

23

call the notes out as you play.

Amazing Grace 〔disc〕 Tr. 7
Teacher Acc.

Hymn

Tenting Tonight 〔disc〕 Tr. 8
Teacher Acc.

Song of the Civil War

Melancholy 〔disc〕 Tr. 9
Teacher Acc.

W. Bay

25

Ledger Lines

When the pitch of a musical sound is below or above the staff, the notes are then placed on or between extra lines called **ledger lines.**

They will be like this:

E F G A B C D   G A B C D E F G

Notes on the A String

Fifth String

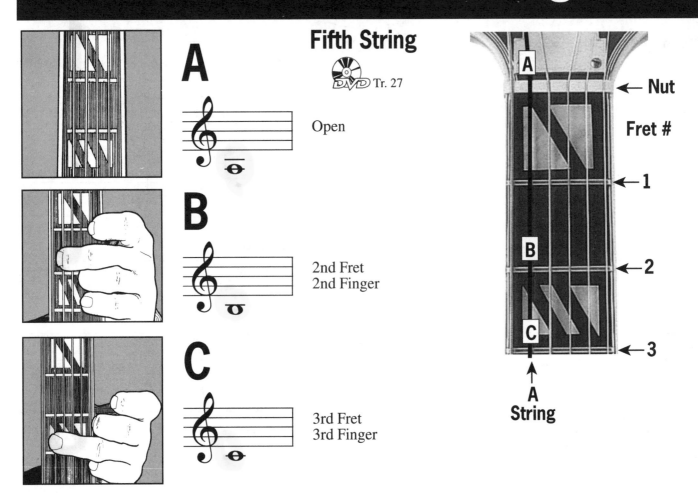

A

Open

B

2nd Fret
2nd Finger

C

3rd Fret
3rd Finger

← Nut

Fret #

← 1

← 2

← 3

↑
A
String

WHOLE NOTES Tr. 28

Count: 1 - 2 - 3 - 4

HALF NOTES Tr. 28

(Rest)

Count: 1 - 2   3 - 4

26

QUARTER NOTES  Tr. 28

Count: 1 2 3 4

(Rest)

Wilderness Trail Tr. 29
Teacher Acc.

Westward Ho! Tr. 29
Teacher Acc.

Chord Waltz Tr. 29
Teacher Acc.

Dotted Quarter Notes

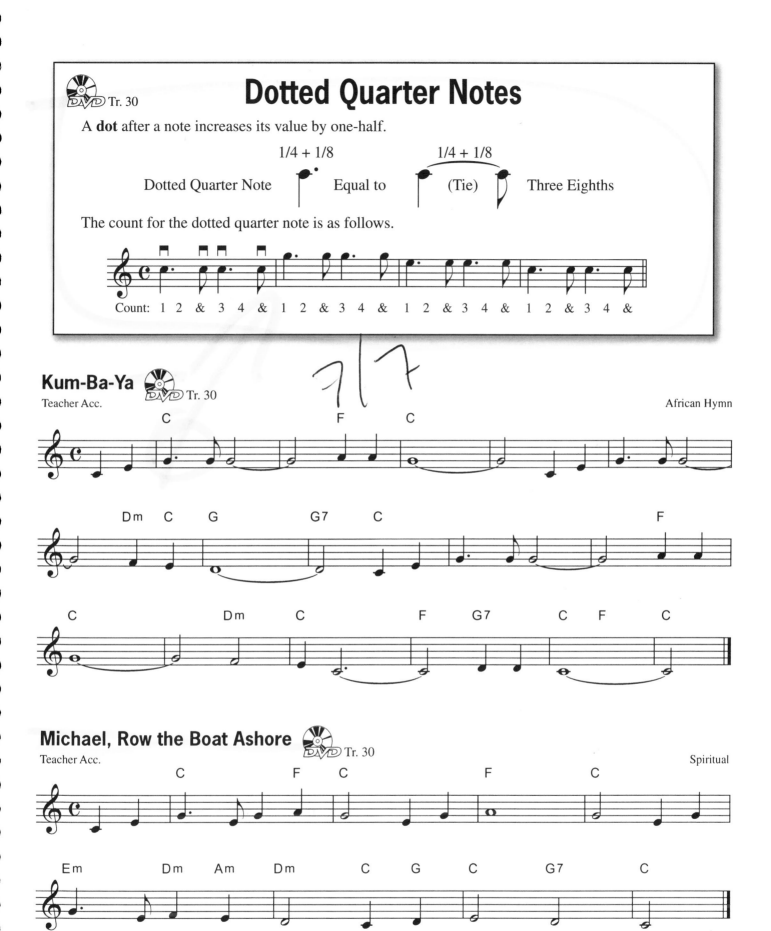

Tr. 30

A **dot** after a note increases its value by one-half.

Dotted Quarter Note   Equal to   (Tie)   Three Eighths

The count for the dotted quarter note is as follows.

Count: 1 2 & 3 4 & 1 2 & 3 4 & 1 2 & 3 4 & 1 2 & 3 4 &

Kum-Ba-Ya
Teacher Acc.   Tr. 30

African Hymn

Michael, Row the Boat Ashore
Teacher Acc.   Tr. 30

Spiritual

Note Review

Call the notes out as you play!

Notes on the E String

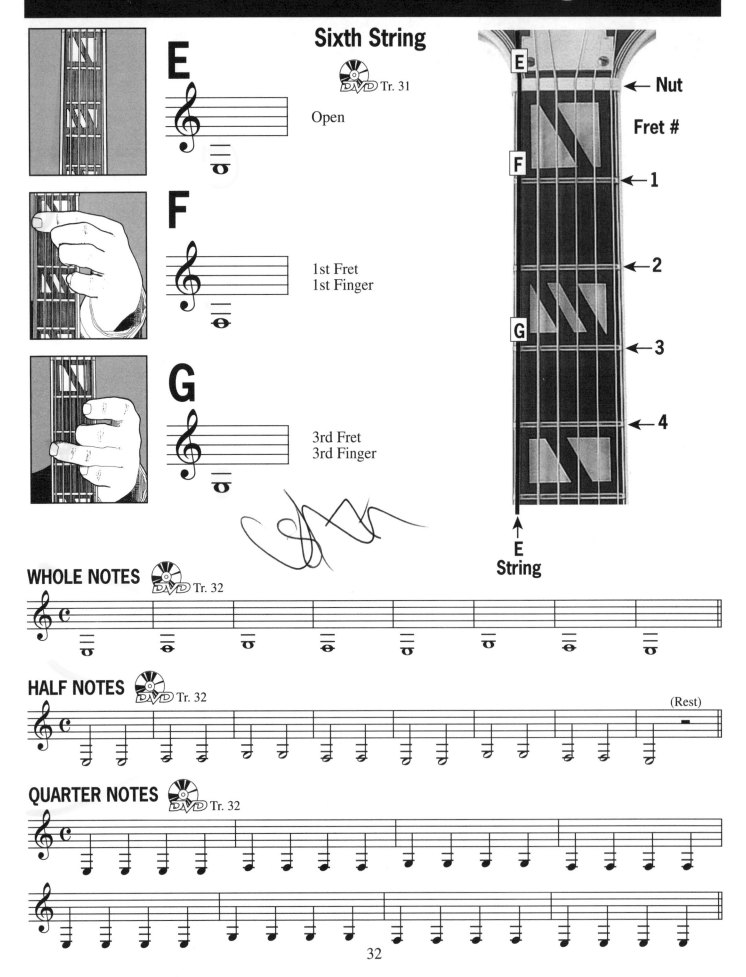

E Open

F 1st Fret
1st Finger

G 3rd Fret
3rd Finger

Sixth String
DVD Tr. 31

Nut

Fret #

← 1

← 2

← 3

← 4

E
String

WHOLE NOTES DVD Tr. 32

HALF NOTES DVD Tr. 32

(Rest)

QUARTER NOTES DVD Tr. 32

Driving Bass
Tr. 33

Low Gear
Teacher Acc.
Tr. 33

Running the Notes
Teacher Acc.
Tr. 33

Introducing the A Note

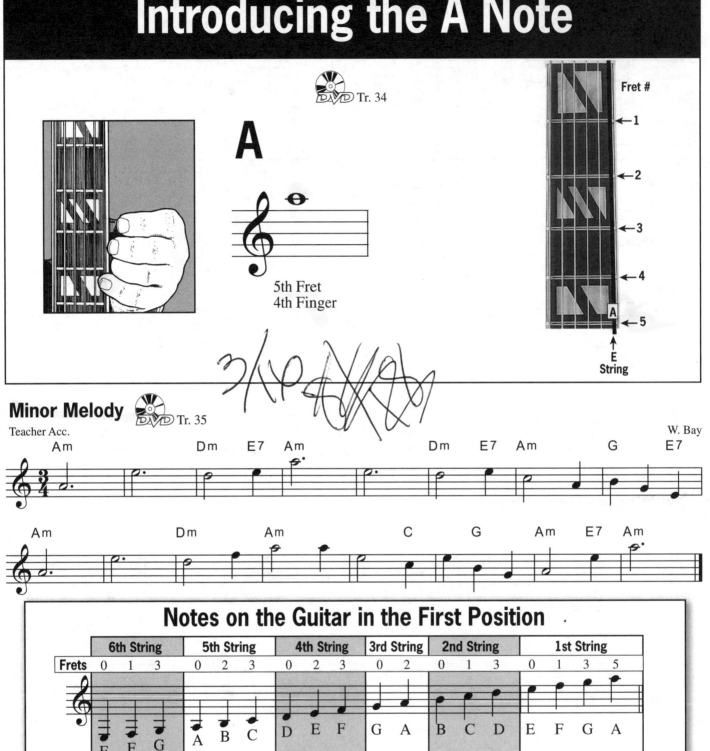

A

5th Fret
4th Finger

Fret #
← 1
← 2
← 3
← 4
A
← 5
↑
E
String

Minor Melody Tr. 35

Teacher Acc.

W. Bay

Am ... Dm E7 Am ... Dm E7 Am ... G E7

Am ... Dm ... Am ... C G ... Am E7 Am

Notes on the Guitar in the First Position

6th String			5th String			4th String			3rd String		2nd String			1st String			
Frets 0	1	3	0	2	3	0	2	3	0	2	0	1	3	0	1	3	5
E	F	G	A	B	C	D	E	F	G	A	B	C	D	E	F	G	A

Hitting on All Six Tr. 35

Teacher Acc.

Mel Bay

34

Playing High A

Smoky Ridge  Tr. 17

Teacher Acc.

Voyage Tr. 18

Teacher Acc.

A Word About Duets

One of the first requisites of a good guitarist is the ability to play well with others. It is with this point in mind that I am stressing the value of duet training.

The modern guitarist has to have the ability to play **solo, harmony,** and **rhythm.**

Duet training will teach the student to perform his or her own part independently without the bewilderment or confusion caused by the rhythm or counterpoint appearing in the second part.

This is one of the most important phases of the student training.

The second part in the following duets will be played by the teacher. The student will be required to play both parts later

Our First Duet Tr. 19
Guitar Duet

| S = Student | T = Teacher |

Arr. by Mel Bay

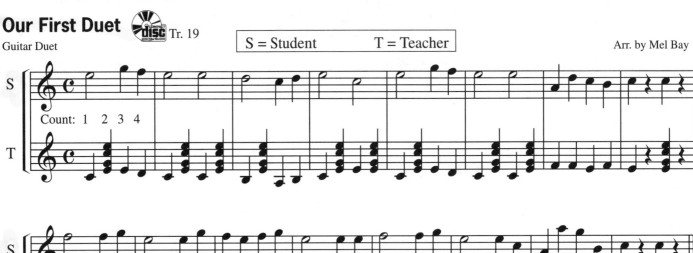

Dots before and after a double bar mean repeat the measures between.

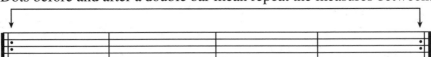

The Repeater Tr. 20
I = 1st Part
II = 2nd Part

The dots placed above and below the third line of the staff at the double bar indicate that the piece is to be repeated.

Two Guitars 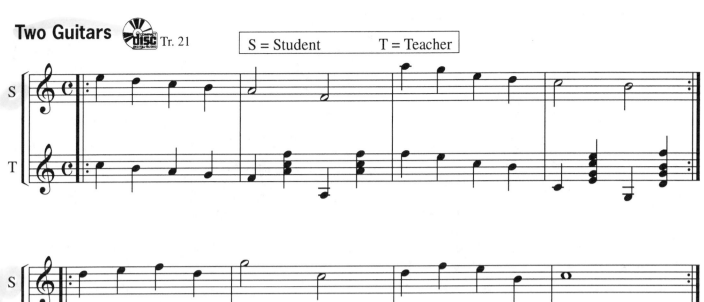 Tr. 21

S = Student   T = Teacher

Sunset  Tr. 22

Chords

A **melody** is a succession of single tones.

A **chord** is a combination of tones sounded together

   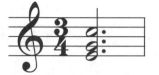

Tones in a Melody   The Same Tones as a Chord

We will construct our chords by playing the chordal tones separately as in a melody and, without raising the fingers, striking them together.

Practice the above etude until it can be played without missing a beat.

*Note that the first finger holds down two notes (C-F) in the second chord.

Chord Songs

Chord March

Autumn

Chording Along

Echoes

Building the F Chord

Two Notes

Three Notes

Four Notes

Four-String Chord Study

We use the same method for building four-string chords as we did in building the three-string chords. Play the chordal tones melodically, holding the fingers down until chord is reached, then strike them together producing the desired chord.

Exercise

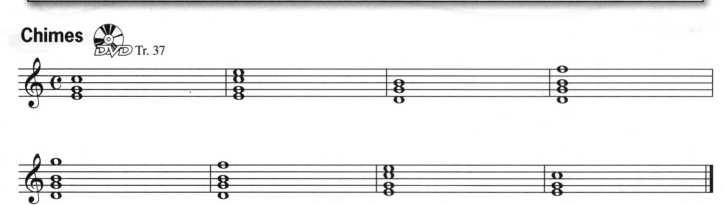

Chimes DVD Tr. 37

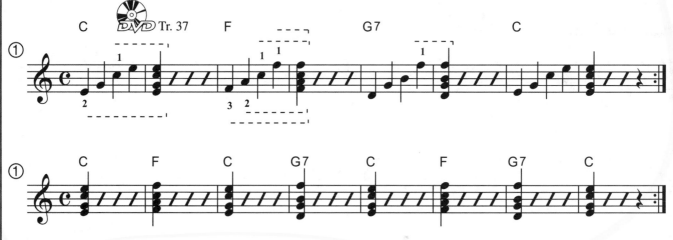

Chord Studies

Bottom Floor

Chord Walk

May Song

Running in the Chord

My Country Tis of Thee
Teacher Acc.

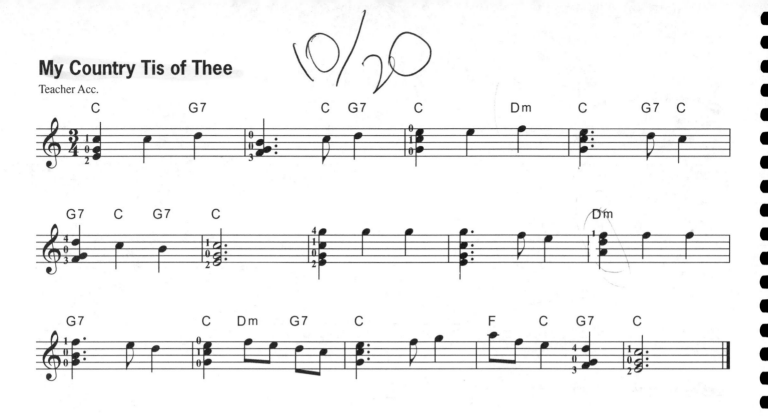

Green Grow the Lilacs
Teacher Acc.

Chord Bouquet
Teacher Acc.

Follow the Leader Tr. 23
Guitar Duet

Arr. by Mel Bay

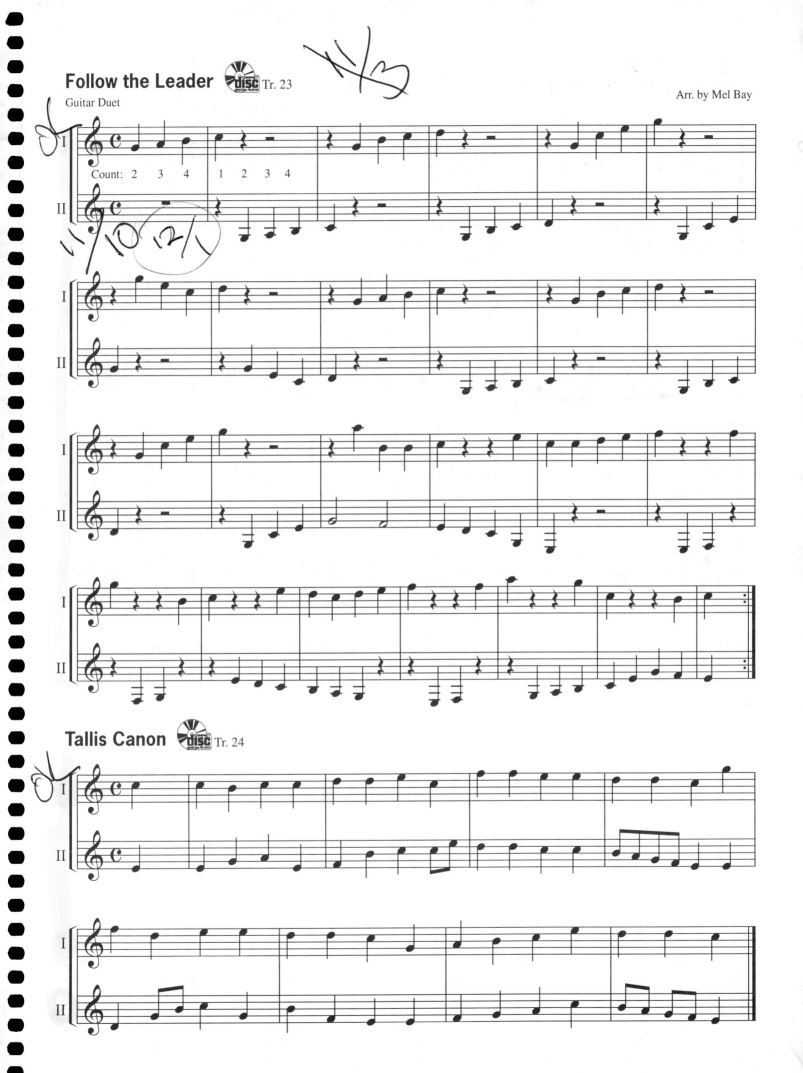

Count: 2 3 4 1 2 3 4

Tallis Canon Tr. 24

43

Bass Solos with Chord Accompaniment

Tr. 38

When playing bass solos with chord accompaniment, you will find the solo with the stems turned downward and the accompaniment with the stems turned upward.

Count: 1 2 3

In the example shown above, you see the dotted half note (E) with the stem downward. It is played on the count of one and held for counts two and three.

The quarter rest over the dotted half note indicates that there is no chord accompanimet at the count of one. The chords with the stems upward are played on counts two and three.

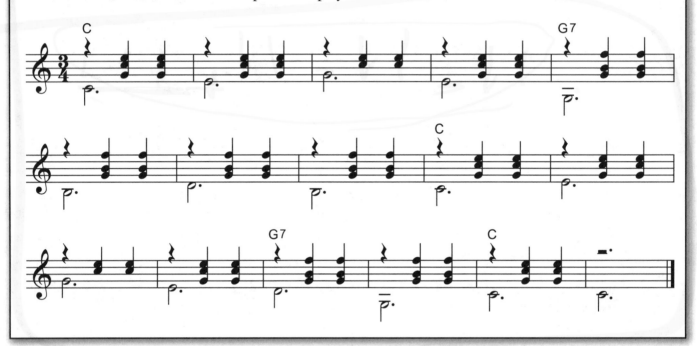

Gliding Along

Tr. 38

Mel Bay

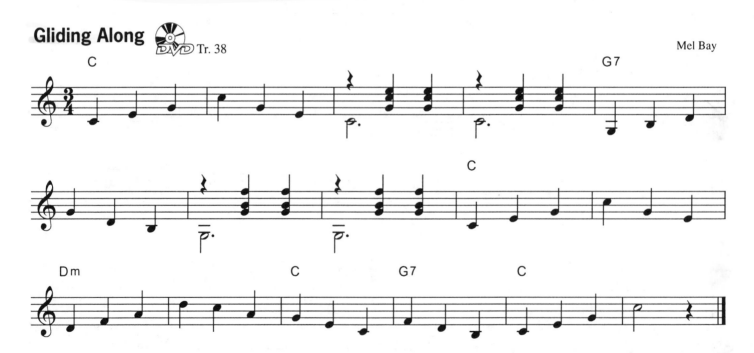

Hymn

Teacher Acc.

Country Waltz

Teacher Acc.

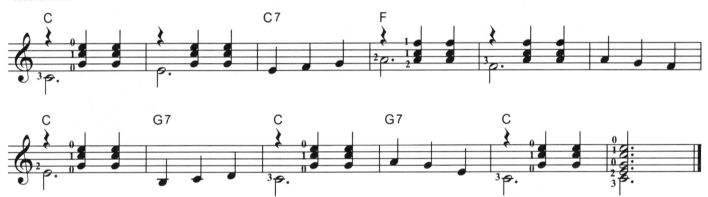

Western Song

Teacher Acc.

The Key of C

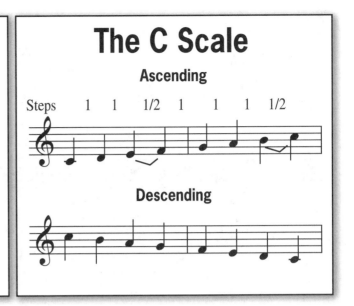

Tr. 39

All music studied so far in this book has been in the key of C. That means that the notes have been taken from the C scale (shown at right) and made into melodies.

It is called the C scale because the first note is a C and we proceed through the musical alphabet until C reappears: C-D-E-F-G-A-B-C.

We will cover the subject of keys and scales more thoroughly in the theory and harmony chapters appearing later in this course.

At present we will deal only with basic fundamentals.

Scale Studies

48

Shenandoah

Tr. 26

Teacher Acc.

Shenandoah – Advanced Version

Teacher Acc.

Blue Bells of Scotland

Tr. 27

Teacher Acc.

Blue Bells of Scotland – Advanced Version

Teacher Acc.

Chords in the Key of C Major

The key of C has three principal chords. They are C, F, and G7.

 Tr. 41

C
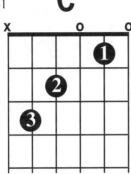

F
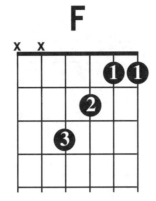

G7
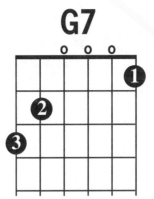

- The circles indicate the position where your fingers should be placed.
- Numerals inside circles indicate the fingers.
- "X" over the strings means that the strings are not to be played.
- "O" over the strings indicates the strings be played open.
- Place fingers in positions indicated by the circles and strike them all together.

Musical Notation of the Chords

Tr. 42

Accompaniment Styles

Tr. 42

Alternate Basses

Tr. 42

In Three-Four Time

51

Chord Studies in C

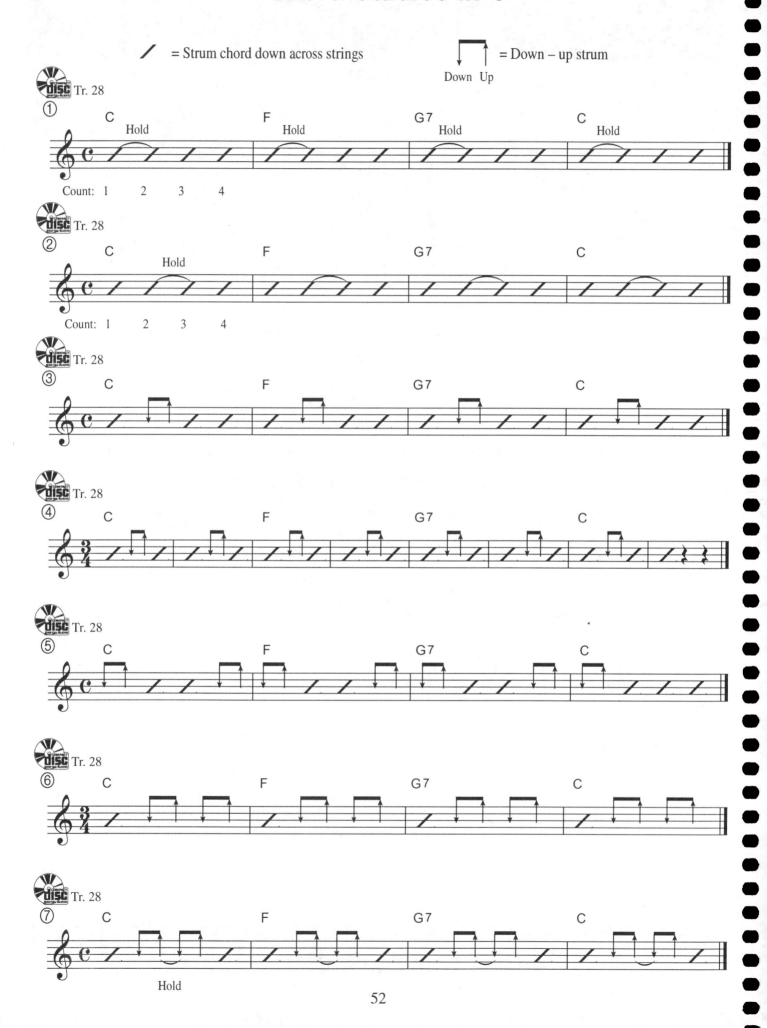

52

A Daily Scale Study  Tr. 29

Count: 1 & 2 & 3 & 4 &

(Repeat ⊓ V ⊓ V)

> The above study should be played slowly with a gradual increase of speed until a moderate tempo has been reached. It is an excellent daily exercise.

Running Around

Teacher Acc.

Home, Home, Can I Forget Thee  Tr. 30

Long, Long Ago Tr. 31

54

Steps

A half-step is the distance from a given tone to the next higher or lower tone. On the guitar, the distance of a half step is one fret.

A whole step consists of two half steps, The distance of a whole step on the guitar is two frets.

The C scale has two half steps. They are between E-F and B-C. Note the distance of one fret between those notes. The distances between C-D, D-E, F-G, G-A, and A-B are whole steps.

Whole steps and half steps are also referred to as whole tones and half tones, We will refer to them as whole steps and half steps.

DVD Tr. 43

Chromatics

The alteration of the pitches of tones is brought about by the use of symbols called **chromatics** (also referred to as **accidentals**).

The Sharp ♯

The sharp placed before a note raises its pitch 1/2 step or one fret.

The Flat ♭

The flat placed before a note lowers its pitch 1/2step or one fret.

The Natural ♮

The natural restores a note to its normal position. It cancels all accidentas previously used.

Sharps

A **sharp** placed in front of a note *raises* the pitch 1/2 step or one fret. Study the notes below

1st String

Remember: when a note is sharped, all notes of that pitch remain sharped throughout the measure unless a **natural sign** (♮) appears. A natural sign cancels a sharp.

1st String Sharps & Naturals

2nd String

3rd String

4th String

5th String

6th String

Walking Guitar  Tr. 44

Flats

A **flat** (♭) placed in front of a note lowers the pitch 1/2 step or one fret. Study the notes below.
A **natural sign** (♮) cancels out the flat.

1st String

2nd String

3rd String

4th String

5th String

6th String

Benny's Flat  Tr. 45

Tempo

Tempo is the rate of speed of a musical composition. Three types of tempos used in this book will be:
Andante: A slow, easy pace. **Moderato:** Moderate. **Allegro:** Lively.

Playtime

Guitar Duet   **Moderato**   Tr. 32

Pleyel
Arr. by Mel Bay

59

The Key of A Minor

 Tr. 46

(Relative to C Major)

- Each major key will have a relative minor key.
- The relative minor scale is built upon the sixth tone of the major scale.
- The key signature of both will be the same.
- The minor scale will have the same number of tones (7) as the major.
- The difference between the two scales is the arrangement of the whole steps and half steps.
- There are three forms of the minor scale: 1) pure or natural, 2) harmonic, 3) melodic.

The A Minor Scale

Natural (Pure)

Harmonic

The 7th tone is raised one half step ascending and descending.  Tr. 47

Melodic  Tr. 49

The 6th and 7th tones are raised one half step ascending and lowered back to their normal pitch descending.

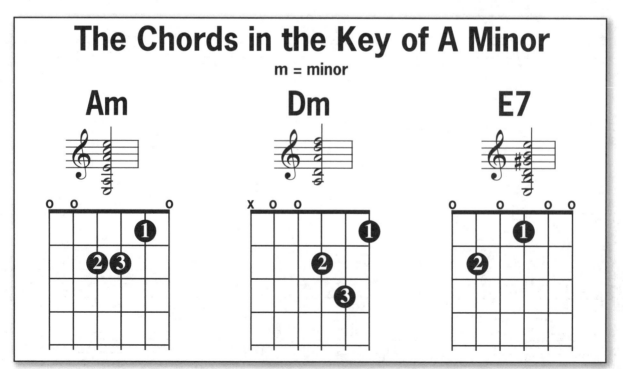

The Chords in the Key of A Minor

m = minor

Am   **Dm**   **E7**

60

Accompaniment Styles in A Minor Tr. 33

Orchestration Style

The Diagonal line (╱) indicates a chord stroke. They will fall only on each beat of the measure.

Repeat the accompaniment exercises until they can be played without missing a beat.

Chord Studies in the Key of Am

Tr. 33   ╱ = Strum chord down across strings   ⌐ = Down – up strum
                                                    Down Up

A Daily Scale Study in A Minor  Tr. 48

Harmonic

(Repeat ⊓ V ⊓ V)

Picking Studies in A Minor

Tr. 48

①

Tr. 48

②

Tr. 48

③

Sailing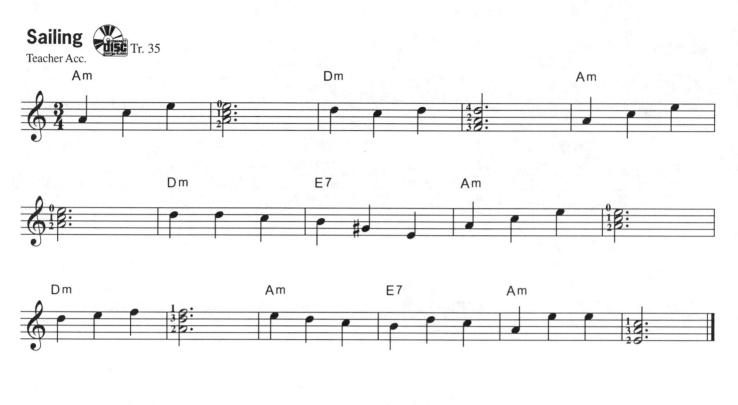
Teacher Acc. Tr. 35

Minor Song
Teacher Acc. Tr. 36

Journey
Teacher Acc. Tr. 37

Hold Sign: 𝄐 This sign placed over or under a note or rest indicates the prolonging of its time value.

Wayfaring Stranger 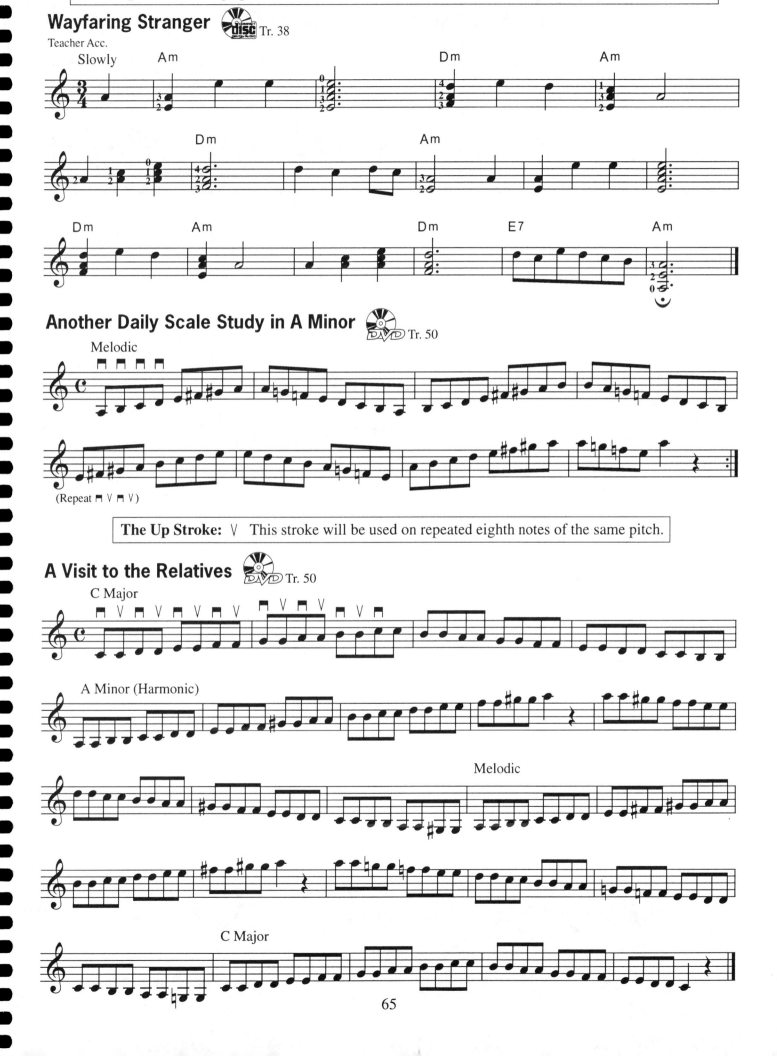 Tr. 38
Teacher Acc.

Another Daily Scale Study in A Minor Tr. 50

(Repeat ⊓ V ⊓ V)

The Up Stroke: V This stroke will be used on repeated eighth notes of the same pitch.

A Visit to the Relatives Tr. 50

65

First and Second Endings

DVD Tr. 51

Sometimes two endings are required in certain selections... one to lead back into a repeated chorus and one to close it. They will be shown like this:

The first time, play the bracketed ending No. 1. Repeat the chorus. The second time, skip the first ending and play ending No. 2.

Shady Glen
DVD Tr. 52

Teacher Acc.

Careless Love
disc Tr. 39

Teacher Acc.

Picking Solos

Foggy Mountain Run  Tr. 40

Teacher Acc.

Cradle Song 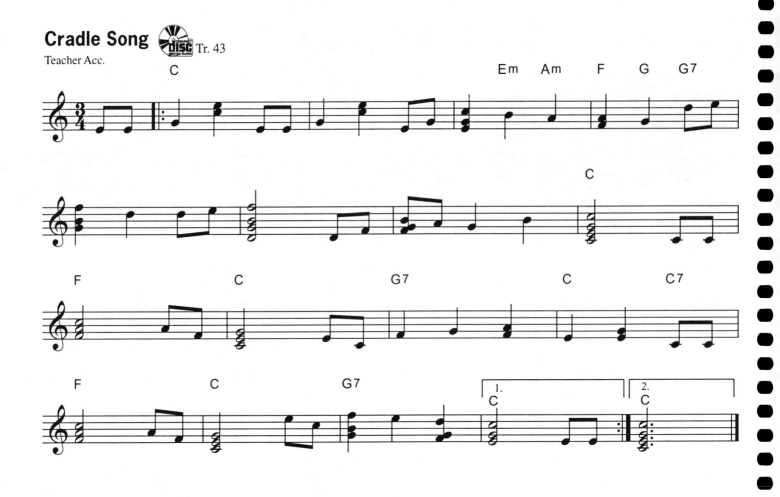 Tr. 43

Teacher Acc.

D.C. al Fine means to go back to the beginning of a piece of music and play until you see the word **Fine** which means "**The End**."

Blue Ridge Trail  Tr. 53

Teacher Acc.

Words Indicating Variations of Tempo

Ritardando or *Ritard (rit.)*...To grow slower   *Accelerando (acc.)*...To increase the speed

Billy's Duet Tr. 44

Lafayette Square Tr. 45

69

Song Without Words

Guitar Duet

Tr. 46

Arr. by Mel Bay

Terry's Tune

Tr. 47

Mel Bay

70

The Key of G

The key of G will have one sharp (F♯). It will be identified by this signature:

The F notes will be played as shown:

6th String	4th String	1st String
2nd Fret	4th Fret	2nd Fret
2nd Finger.	4th Finger.	2nd Finger.

The G Scale

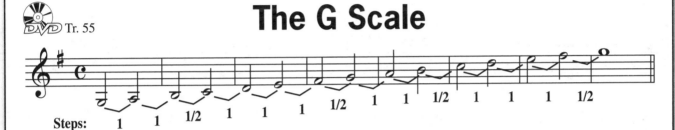

Note that, in order to have the half steps falling between the seventh and eighth degrees of the scale, the F must be sharped. Our major scale pattern is then correct (1-1-1/2-1-1-1-1/2 Steps).

A Daily Drill  Tr. 48

Picking Studies in G  Tr. 48

71

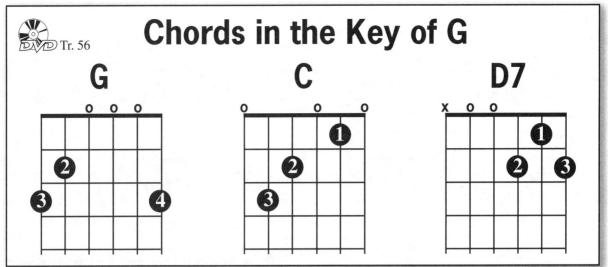

Chords in the Key of G

Tr. 56

G   C   D7

Accompaniment Styles in the Key of G   Tr. 49

73

G Boogie
Teacher Acc.
Tr. 57

In the Evening by the Moonlight
Tr. 50

The following etude introduces the notes D and B being played together. This is done by playing the note D with the first finger on the third fret of the second string and playing the note B with the second finger on the fourth fret of the **third string.**

Etude
Tr. 51

Fine

D.C. al Fine

Two-Four Time

This sign  indicates **two-four** time.

2 – beats per measure.
4 – a quarter note receives one beat.

Two-four time will have two beats per measure with the quarter note receiving one beat.

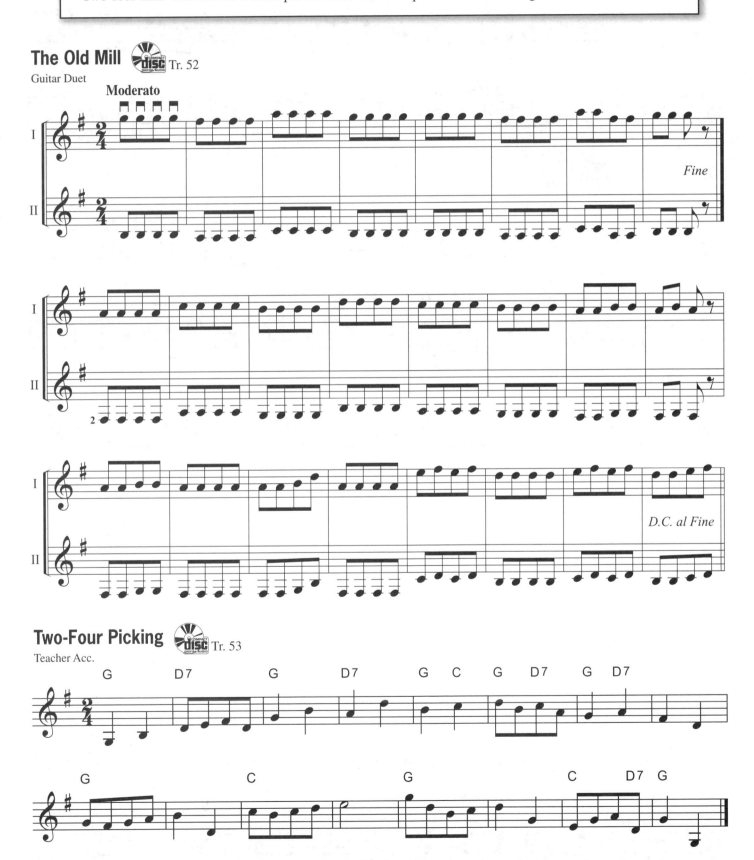

The Old Mill 💿 Tr. 52

Guitar Duet

Moderato

Fine

2

D.C. al Fine

Two-Four Picking 💿 Tr. 53

Teacher Acc.

75

A Scale Study 💿 Tr. 54

Count: 1   2   &   3   &   4   &

(Repeat ⊓ V ⊓ V)

Opening Day 💿 Tr. 55

G   C   D7   G   D7

C   D7   G   C   G   D7   G   D7   G
                                                                     1.

D7   G   C   G   C   G   C   G
2.
Fine

D7   G   C   G   C   G   D7   G

D.C. al Fine

A Serenade 💿 Tr. 56
Guitar Solo   Mel Bay

Moderato   G   D7   D9   D9   D7

G°   G   G7   C   C#°

D7   D9   D7   G   D7   G
              4   4   1.   2.

76

Austrian Hymn

Guitar Duet

Tr. 57

Haydn

Home on the Range

Guitar Solo

Tr. 58

> = Accent

77

The Little Prince

Guitar Duet

Tr. 59

Mazas
Arr. by Mel Bay

Andante

Carry Me Back to Old Virginny

Guitar Solo

Tr. 60

Bland
Arr. by Mel Bay

Andante

* The wavy line before the last chord means to glide the pick slowly over the strings, producing a harp-like effect. The musical term for this is **Quasi Arpi**.

The Key of E Minor

(Relative to G Major)

 Tr. 58

The key of E minor will have the same key signature as G major.

Two E Minor Scales

Harmonic

Melodic

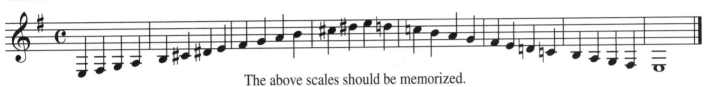

The above scales should be memorized.

Picking Studies Tr. 61

①

② Tr. 61

③ Tr. 61

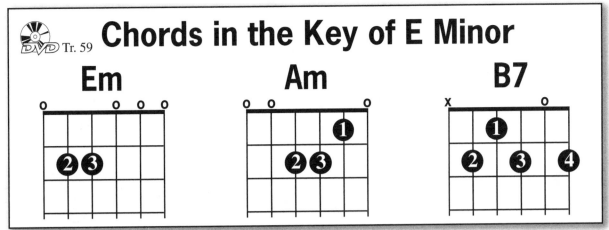

Chords in the Key of E Minor
DVD Tr. 59

Em   **Am**   **B7**

Accompaniment Styles in the Key of E Minor
CD Tr. 63

* This sign (℅) means that the previous measure is to be repeated.

Orchestration Styles

Chord Studies
CD Tr. 63

Morning Song 🎵 Tr. 60

American Folk Hymn

Cindy 💿 Tr. 64

Night Song 💿 Tr. 65

Sor
Arr. by Mel Bay

East River

Goblins

A Chord Review

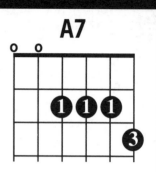

A7

- The key of C has six chords. They are C, F, G7, Am, Dm, and E7.
- The latter three are in the relative minor key but use the key signature of C.
- All "outside" chords are **Accidental Chords**.
- The most commonly used of these chords are D7 and A7.
- The six chords found in the key of G are G, C, D7, Em, Am, and B7.
- The most common accidental chords found in the key of G are A7 and E7.

Spotting the accidentals in the various chords will facilitate the reading of them... for example:

- B7 will have a D♯   • E7 will have a G♯   • A7 will have a C♯   • D7 will have a F♯

In the following studies, you will see how they appear.

Lament 🎵 Tr. 68

Guitar Solo

Mel Bay

Maytime

Guitar Duet

Wanhall-Bay

Tone

Music is composed of sounds pleasant to the ear.

Sound maybe made from **noise** or **tone.**

Noise is made by irregular vibrations such as would be caused by striking a table with a hammer, the shot of a gun, or slapping two stones together.

Tone is produced by regular vibrations as would be caused by drawing a bow over the strings of a violin, striking the strings of a guitar, or blowing through a wind instrument such as a trumpet.

A tone has four characteristics ... **pitch, duration, dynamics, and timbre**.

> **Pitch**: the highness or lowness of a tone.
> **Duration**: the length of a tone.
> **Dynamics**: the force or power of a tone (loudness or softness).
> **Timbre**: quality of the tone.

A note represents the pitch and duration of a tone.

Dynamics are indicated by words such as:

> *Pianissimo* . . . . (**pp**) . . . . very soft
> *Piano* . . . . (**p**) . . . . soft
> *Mezzo piano* . . . . (**mp**) . . . . medium soft
> *Mezzo forte* . . . . (**mf**) . . . . medium loud
> *Forte* . . . . (**f**) . . . . very loud

Timbre depends upon the skill of the performer plus the quality of the instrument which is being played.

Rondo
Guitar Duet

Tr. 70

Student should play both parts

Mazas, Op. 85
Arr. by Mel Bay

Allegro

Sor's Waltz Tr. 71

Arr. by Mel Bay

Bluegrass Waltz Tr. 72

Mel Bay

Running the Thirds in G  Tr. 73

A Little Bit of Hanon Tr. 74

Mel Bay

Southern Fried Tr. 75

Swing Feeling

Mel Bay

G   F   F# G   F   F#   G   F#   G   F   F# G   F   F#   G   G° D7

Count: 1 & 2 & 3 & 4 &   Count: 1 & 2 & 3 & 4 &

G   F   F# G   D7   C   G°   G   D7   G   D7   G